FABULOUS FLAVOURS

Brunch • High Tea • Cocktails

MW01699646

FLAVOURS

A-81, Sector V
Noida-201301, Uttar Pradesh, India

First Published by Brijbasi Art Press Ltd. 2006
Reprint 2007

Text: EASA (External Affairs [Ministry's] Spouses Association)

Photography: Karan Khanna

Design: Arun Joshi

Edited by Nasima Aziz

Project Coordinator: Veena Baswani

ISBN 81-8385-082-0

Processed, Printed and bound at
©Brijbasi Art Press Ltd.
E-46/11, Okhla Industrial Area, Phase-II
New Delhi-110020, India.

FABULOUS FLAVOURS

Brunch • High Tea • Cocktails

by

External Affairs [Ministry's]

Spouses Association, New Delhi

BRIJBASI

FLAVOURS

Photography: Karan Khanna

contents

introduction

As one of the fund-raising projects for EASA's Charitable Trust, the cookbook committee has put together a set of cookbooks: *Fabulous Flavours — Non-Vegetarian; Vegetarian; and Brunch ✦ High Tea ✦ Cocktails.* For us, the members of EASA, the External Affairs Ministry's Spouses Association, food and entertaining becomes a major focus when we are posted to our Embassies abroad. We are always collecting recipes and cooking tips that will help us to entertain those 30 'short-notice' dinner guests and those hundreds of invitees to the National Day Reception.

We published our first collection of recipes, *Silver Spoons,* in 1994, which became a learning manual for many a young wife on her first assignment abroad. Recipes have been a popular section of our in-house magazines over the years; the food stall is invariably a money spinner at the charity bazaars that we organise in the capital cities of the world; and in New Delhi, the annual Global Gourmet Gala, in which foreign Embassies participate with EASA, has become our biggest fund-raising event of the year.

Fabulous Flavours takes the best recipes from *Silver Spoons* and from the magazines to make a comprehensive collection; these recipes have been passed down from senior colleagues to their juniors within the Embassy Family; they have travelled to the next place of posting and have been shared with other colleagues, making this a valuable culinary inheritance.

The Association was registered in 1971, though informal meetings used to take place even earlier. Our magazine, called the EASA Annual, is a sizable and substantial journal that helps us stay in touch with each other in places that are scattered in literally every country of the globe. Through the magazine and the monthly meetings of the Association in New Delhi we provide practical and emotional support to

each other, discuss common problems and find solutions for them.

EASA's Charitable Trust, registered in 1978, has helped numerous institutions and individuals all over the country. It is managed by a volunteer committee of EASA's members who select the charities to be assisted, follow up on the donations made, and rouse the members to do their bit towards fund raising.

To quote from an article in a recent issue of the Annual: "Very often, sitting thousands of miles away from home, bereft of the strength that one can draw from our near and dear ones, we have to look for strength within us.

We are that crucial cog-in-the-wheel which keeps the show going on the road, smoothly and effectively. But somewhere along the line, between arranging the perfect dinner and playing the charming hostess, is the lady who needs to do things for herself."

EASA provides a forum where all our voices can be heard; it helps us to find our own individual identity, distinct from our role as the spouse of a diplomat.

Metric measurements have been used – kilograms (kg), grams (g), litres (l) and millilitres (ml).
Cups, tablespoons (tbsp) and teaspoons (tsp) are level unless specified.

EASA's magazines are not only a storehouse of the best recipes, they are a forum for thought-provoking discussions, frank opinions, fiery debates, humorous experiences and poignant memoirs. Here we have selected quotations from articles, spanning almost 2 decades, written by our members on the pros and cons of Foreign Service Life:

"People call us lucky, look at us with envy, all because we are globe-trotters. We get to live in exotic places, travel extensively, lead a great lifestyle and hop in and out of parties. Our children have accents and go to international schools. But this is only one side of the coin. What about the pains of a nomadic life, of making and breaking friendships, of pulling the kids out of a secure environment and placing them in a new one with a fresh set of rules and disciplines, of packing and unpacking? Yet another torture is loneliness. We miss familiar surroundings and family occasions – both happy and sad, and the comfort of an extended family. Can living in an exotic place compensate for the loneliness of having a first delivery far away from home in unknown surroundings? We do take pride in doing everything to perfection and doing our bit for our nation but we do not want to be taken for granted."

"Of course it is not all bad! Let's face it – we have seen new places, widened our horizons, met any number of very interesting people. We are able to churn out perfect meals in a matter of hours, after recipes have been exchanged, tried out, discussed to the minutest detail, till one has got it just right. When all has been planned, we are then to sit in the drawing room, looking as though we have nothing to do with all the events of the past hours in the kitchen. Has the maid burnt the rice? Has the bake charred to a crisp? We organise bazaars and fashion shows for charity, entertain Indian travellers . . . . Imagine our shock when we return home to discover that our value in the job market has plummeted, we

have missed out on years of work experience, and nobody is at all interested in how to make paneer with powdered milk!"

"The scale on which we have to entertain, specially on National Day and other similar occasions, is mind-boggling. Coming as most of us do from small nuclear families, the prospect of entertaining by the hundreds is a daunting task. Hours are spent on planning, calculating quantities of ingredients for large numbers, juggling around with all available crockery, cutlery and linen, shopping in bulk from the most economical stores and generally putting life on hold till the 'do' is over. The sheer physical stamina required to see such an event through – holding forth with endless guests, praying that the food does not run short, hoping that there is no crisis in the kitchen, propping oneself up on groaning feet, nursing a smile on an aching face – all in the honourable cause of the motherland, surely there is a price to be paid!"

"From the onset, the rules of Diplomacy were well defined for the Foreign Service officer, but for his spouse it was a bewildering world. The process of learning began immediately. One grasped that the only home away from home was the Embassy. In fact, it became your family, your *maika*. There was somebody from the Embassy to receive you, to take you home, to tell you where to get a bag of wholewheat flour, *aata*, your first and foremost requirement. Thus began a dialogue which transcended regional feelings and subsequently helped one to find one's bearings as one joined the diplomatic tribe.

As a young officer enthused with his new role as the country's representative abroad, my husband insisted on inviting people home on a routine basis, gathering them from different strata of society and feeding them with authentic

Indian food, cooked by his dear wife, who managed to churn our dishes by trial and error.

The Foreign Service is one of the rare services where the wife has an equally challenging role. The diplomat does not function as a single unit but as a double entity. By the time the spouse is one of the senior-most members of the Embassy, she has learnt how to get things done: how to cope with the pressures of demanding houseguests and the tantrums of domestic staff. She has perfected the skill of organising a VIP visit, where she has a key role to play. In short, the role of the Foreign Service wife is not clearcut but gradually evolves over a period and every spouse can lend individuality to it and contribute to her husband's career in her own unique way."

kitchen basics

How to dry-roast ingredients

Although any frying pan may be used for dry-roasting, an iron griddle, *tawa*, retains the heat well and is ideal. Place the ingredient – whole spices, spice powders, gram flour, nuts or semolina (*suji*) – on the hot *tawa* and cook on medium heat, stirring, or shaking the pan, until evenly browned. As soon as the ingredient is a few shades darker than it was to start with, and emits a fragrant aroma, tip it onto a tray.

Drained Yogurt/Hung Yogurt

Draining the water out of yogurt makes it extra-thick and creamy. The traditional way is to tie it into a bundle in a piece of muslin or cheesecloth, hang it up for several hours and allow it to drip. A quick way to do this is to rub the yogurt through an extremely fine nylon sieve. Thick yogurt can often be used as a substitute for mayonnaise in dressings and dips.

White Urad Dal

Skinless black gram, *dhuli safed urad dal* is sometimes used along with whole spice seeds as an ingredient in tempering oil; it is fried till the colour changes from white to pink, after that it burns. It may be soaked and ground to make a batter for dumplings and fritters and it can also be cooked like any other dal.

Mint-Coriander Chutney

1/4 cup tightly packed mint leaves
1 cup tightly packed coriander leaves
2 tsp dried mango powder (*amchur*)
2 green chillies
salt to taste
water as required

Put all the ingredients in a blender and blend into a smooth paste, adding water to give the chutney a thick, sauce-like consistency.

Tamarind Chutney (Sonth)

100 g tamarind
2 cups hot water
100 g sugar
1 tsp cumin seeds, roasted, powdered
1/2 tsp red chilli powder
1/2 tsp black salt
salt to taste

Soak the tamarind in the water for 30 minutes; rub to loosen the pulp from the fibres; strain the pulp into a pan, discarding the fibres; add the sugar, cumin

and red chilli powders, black salt and salt and boil until the chutney is reduced to the thickness of ketchup. This chutney will keep well for several days. Diced, ripe mangos, sliced bananas or grapes may be stirred into a bowl of chutney while serving.

Fluffy Cucumber Dressing

1 cup heavy cream, whipped
1/2 tsp salt
1/4 tsp paprika
2-3 tbsp lemon juice
1/2 cups mayonnaise
1 cup peeled, minced cucumber, drained

Combine everything and serve immediately. Makes 2 1/2 cups.

Lemon-Orange Dressing

1/3 cup sugar
1 tsp salt
1 tsp paprika
1/4 cup orange juice
2 1/2 tsp lemon juice
1 tsp grated onions
1 cup salad oil

Put everything in a jar; close tightly, shake vigorously to blend. Makes 1 3/4 cups.

Chinese Salad Dressing

2 tbsp sugar
4 tbsp white vinegar
2 tbsp sesame oil
4 tbsp olive oil
2 tbsp soya sauce
1/2 tsp pepper
1 tsp salt

Put everything in a jar; close tightly, shake vigorously to blend. Makes 1/2 cup.

brunch

Spinach and Mushroom Quiche

PREPARATION TIME: 25 MINUTES
COOKING TIME: 30 MINUTES
BAKING TIME: 30 – 40 MINUTES
SERVES 4

1. Place the spinach in a non-stick pan; cover and cook on medium heat – it steams and softens in the water it releases. When it is tender, remove and drain.
2. Melt the butter in a shallow pan and sauté the mushrooms on high heat.
3. Spread the spinach and mushrooms over the pie crust.
4. Beat the eggs lightly in a bowl; blend in the cheese, milk, cream, salt, pepper, nutmeg and Worcestershire sauce; pour over the spinach-mushroom mixture.
5. Bake the quiche in a preheated oven at 180C/350 F for 30 minutes or until the egg mixture (the custard) is just set. Allow the quiche to cool and settle for a few minutes before serving.

a 23 cm (9") pie crust, ready-made
500 g spinach, washed, drained, chopped
200 g mushrooms, sliced

butter as required
3 eggs
$^{2}/_{3}$ cup cheddar cheese, grated
$^{3}/_{4}$ cup milk
$^{1}/_{2}$ cup cream
salt to taste
1 tsp pepper, freshly ground
$^{1}/_{2}$ tsp nutmeg, freshly grated
2 tsp Worcestershire sauce

Spaghetti Bolognese

PREPARATION TIME: 10 MINUTES
COOKING TIME: 40 MINUTES
SERVES 4

500 g spaghetti (fresh or packaged)
750 g minced mutton (*keema*)

3 tbsp olive oil
2 medium onions, chopped
6 cloves garlic, chopped
3 large tomatoes, chopped
2 tbsp tomato purée
salt and pepper to taste
1/4 tsp dried basil
1/4 tsp dried oregano
1/2 cup water
60 g Parmesan cheese, grated
black pepper, freshly ground, to taste

1. Heat 2 tbsp of the olive oil in a non-stick pan, add the onions and garli and sauté until soft. Add the minced mutton and sauté on high heat till it browns. Stir in the tomatoes, tomato purée, salt, pepper, basil, oregano and water; cover and cook for 20 to 25 minutes or until the meat sauce is fully cooked and thick; reserve.
2. Use a large pan, preferably a pasta pan that makes draining easier; fill it with water and bring to a boil; add the spaghetti, a pinch of salt and the remaining olive oil. Boil the spaghetti for 10 minutes on high heat or until the spaghetti is *al dente*; drain.
3. Transfer the spaghetti onto a warm dish and pour the meat sauce over it; sprinkle the top with the Parmesan cheese and pepper; serve hot.

COOK'S NOTE
If the spaghetti is over cooked it will become soft and limp; stop the cooking when it is tender but still firm between the teeth, described by the Italian phrase, *al dente*.

Super Salad Niçoise

PREPARATION TIME: 20 MINUTES
SERVES 4

For the dressing:
4 tbsp olive oil
2 tbsp white wine vinegar
salt and pepper to taste

500 g new potatoes
500 g French beans
4-5 spring onions, chopped
a handful of salad leaves
10 black olives
4-5 anchovies (optional)
1 tin tuna chunks
4 tomatoes, quartered
4 hard-boiled eggs, halved

1. Put the ingredients for the dressing in a jar with a tight-fitting lid and shake to blend.
2. Boil the potatoes, cool and quarter.
3. Trim the French beans, boil and cool.
4. Place the potatoes and spring onions in a salad bowl; pour in half the dressing, mix and set aside for 10 minutes. Add the beans, salad leaves, olives and anchovies and toss together. Place tuna chunks, tomatoes and eggs on top of the salad and pour the rest of the dressing over it.

COOK'S NOTE
The French city of Nice has given its name to this traditional salad.

Fruit in Honey-Yogurt

PREPARATION TIME: 20 MINUTES
CHILLING TIME: 1 HOUR
SERVES 4

2 cups thick yogurt
1/2 cup honey

4 cups fresh fruit, diced
1 1/2 tbsp lemon juice
3 tbsp ginger, preserved in sugar syrup
1 tsp cinnamon powder, to garnish

1. Put the yogurt in a bowl, add the honey and stir till smooth and creamy
2. Put the fruit in another bowl, stir in the lemon juice and ginger.
3. Make individual servings in dessert bowls, alternating layers of fruit and yogurt; garnish with cinnamon powder; serve chilled.

COOK'S NOTE

- Ginger that has been preserved in sugar syrup is commercially available in bottles.
- Crystallised or candied ginger may be used as a substitute; this is also commercially available. To make it at home, simmer thinly sliced fresh ginger in water for 20 to 30 minutes; drain; weigh and add an equal amount of sugar and a few teaspoons water; cook, stirring, until the ginger is transparent and dry; toss in castor sugar to get well coated and store in an airtight jar

Sambhar (Spicy Dal with Vegetables)

(see p. 28 c)

PREPARATION TIME: 15 MINUTES
COOKING TIME: 25 MINUTES
SERVES 4

For the sambhar masala:
1 tsp fenugreek seeds (*methi*)
2 tbsp red gram (*toor/arhar* dal)
2 tbsp split Bengal gram (*chana* dal)
4 tbsp coriander seeds
5-6 dry red chillies
1/2 tsp asafoetida (*hing*)

1 cup red gram (*toor/arhar* dal)
6 cups water
2 cups mixed vegetables, diced
3 green chillies, slit
2 tbsp tamarind pulp,
dissolved in 1/2 cup water
1/2 tsp turmeric powder
salt to taste
1 tbsp sugar
2 tbsp of the *sambhar* masala
Tempering:
1 tbsp oil
1 tsp mustard seeds
1 tsp skinless black gram
(*dhuli safed urad* dal)
1/4 tsp asafoetida (*hing*)
a few curry leaves
2 tbsp coriander leaves, chopped

1. Dry-roast (see p. 12) all the ingredients for the *sambhar* masala, each separately, on a hot griddle, *tawa*; grind to make a fine powder; store in an airtight bottle.
2. Place the red gram in a pressure cooker with 2 cups of the water and cook until tender; mash the dal against the sides of the pan; keep aside.
3. Put the vegetables in a large pan along with the rest of the water, tamarind, turmeric powder, salt and sugar and cook until the vegetables are tender; add the *sambhar* masala and the reserved dal and simmer for 10 minutes.
4. Heat the oil in a small pan, add the mustard seeds and *urad* dal; when the mustard seeds start to splutter add the asafoetida and the curry leaves; pour into the *sambhar* and simmer the *sambhar* for 5 more minutes; garnish with coriander leaves and serve hot.

COOK'S NOTE
- Ready-made *sambhar* masala is commercially available.
- Any fresh vegetables may be used, including drumsticks, onions, button onions, tomatoes and thick slices of radish.

Upama (Savoury Semolina)

(see p. 28 g)

PREPARATION TIME: 10 MINUTES
COOKING TIME: 10 MINUTES
SERVES 4

3/4 cup semolina (*suji, rawa*)

3 tbsp oil
6 cashew nuts
2 tbsp peanuts
1 tsp mustard seeds
1 1/2 tbsp split Bengal gram (*chana* dal)
1 tsp skinless black gram (*dhuli safed urad* dal)
a few curry leaves
1" ginger, minced
4 green chillies, finely chopped
1 large onion, chopped
1 carrot, diced
1/4 cup peas
salt to taste
1 3/4 cups water
1 tbsp lemon juice

1. Dry-roast (see p. 12) the semolina on a hot griddle, *tawa,* till it begins to smell fragrant; remove and keep aside.
2. Heat the oil in a pan, add the cashew nuts and peanuts and sauté until golden; remove and keep aside.
3. In the same oil add the mustard seeds, *chana* and *urad* dals; when the mustard seeds start to splutter add the curry leaves, ginger and green chillies; stir in the onions, carrots and peas; sprinkle with salt.
4. Add the water and bring to a boil; add the semolina, stirring continuously to prevent lumps. Reduce the heat, cover and cook for 2 minutes then turn off the heat but leave covered for another 2 minutes. Sprinkle with lemon juice, transfer to a serving dish and garnish with the reserved cashew nuts and peanuts; serve hot.

Idlis (Steamed Dumplings)

PREPARATION TIME: 1 HOUR
SOAKING TIME: 4 HOURS
FERMENTATION TIME: OVERNIGHT
COOKING TIME: 30 MINUTES
SERVES 4

1 cup skinless black gram (*dhuli safed urad* dal)
3 cups parboiled rice (*sela chawal*)
salt to taste

coconut chutney to serve (see p. 29)
sambhar to serve (see p. 22)

an *idli*-making stand and steamer

1. Wash the *urad* dal and rice and soak in separate bowls for 4 hours; drain.
2. Put the *urad* dal and rice, each separately, in a grinder and grind to a fine paste; mix the two pastes together in a large bowl, add salt and stir till well blended; set aside to ferment overnight.
3. Place one serving spoon of the batter in each *idli* mould in the stand; fill all the moulds. A stand with smaller moulds makes cocktail-size *idlis*. Place the stand in the steamer, filling water below the level of the idlis, and steam for 10 to 12 minutes or until the *idlis* are firm; remove the *idlis* from the moulds and make the next batch in the same way. To freeze, put *idlis* in zip-lock bags. To heat, open the bag, sprinkle a little water and close, leaving a small opening for steam to escape. Microwave the bag for 4 to 5 minutes or till the *idlis* are piping hot.

COOK'S NOTE
Uthapams, pancakes, can be made with over-fermented *idli* batter. Stir 2 tbsp flour into the batter and make a pancake on a hot griddle, using a little oil; sprinkle the top with diced onions and tomatoes; serve with the same chutneys as the *idlis.*

Vadas (Deep-fried Fritters)

PREPARATION TIME: 1 HOUR
SOAKING TIME: 4 – 6 HOURS
COOKING TIME: 30 MINUTES
SERVES 4

1 cup skinless black gram (*dhuli safed urad* dal)

water as required
2 medium onions, chopped
1/2 tsp cumin seeds
2 green chillies, finely chopped
1″ ginger, minced
1 tsp salt

oil to deep-fry

coconut chutney to serve (p. 29)
sambhar to serve (p. 22)

1. Wash the dal and soak it for 4 to 6 hours; drain; put it in a grinder and grind to make a thick batter, using a little water.
2. Transfer the batter to a bowl, add the onions, cumin seeds, green chillie ginger and salt and mix will. Make doughnut-shaped patties, *vadas*, using wet hands to prevent the batter from sticking.
3. Heat the oil in a wok, *karhai*, add the *vadas* in batches and deep-fry till golden and crisp on the outside and cooked through to the inside; remo and drain; serve with coconut chutney and *sambhar*.

COOK'S NOTE
- *Urad* dal is difficult to grind and needs some patience; if too much water is added the *vadas* absorb a lot of oil during frying.
- To freeze, half-fry the *vadas*, cool and store in zip-lock bags. To serve, defrost and deep-fry the *vadas* in hot oil till golden.

c
b
d
e
f
a
h
g

Accompaniments for a south Indian Thali

Onion Chutney

2 tbsp oil
1/2 cup split Bengal gram (*chana* dal)
4 dry red chillies
3 medium onions, chopped
2 tbsp tamarind pulp
salt to taste
Tempering: (optional)
1 tsp oil
1/2 tsp mustard seeds
1 red chilli, halved
6 curry leaves

1. Heat the oil in a pan, add the *chana* dal and dry red chillies and fry until they deepen in colour; add the onions and sauté till they turn transparent; cool; place in a blender along with the tamarind and salt and grind to a fine paste; transfer the chutney to a bowl.
2. Heat the oil in a small pan, add the mustard seeds and dry red chilli; when the mustard seeds begin to splutter, add the curry leaves; pour over the chutney; serve with *idlis* or *vadas*.

Coconut Chutney

2 cups coconut, grated
1/2 cup peanuts, dry-roasted (see p. 12)
6-8 green chillies
2 cloves garlic
1/2 tsp cumin seeds
salt to taste
water as required
Tempering:
1 tsp oil
1/2 tsp mustard seeds
1/4 tsp cumin seeds
1 dry red chilli, halved
a few curry leaves

1. Put the coconut, peanuts, green chillies, garlic, cumin seeds and salt in a blender and grind to a fine paste, adding a little water; transfer the chutney to a bowl.
2. Heat the oil in a small pan, add the mustard and cumin seeds and dry red chilli; when the mustard seeds start to splutter add the curry leaves and pour over the chutney; serve immediately with *idlis* or *vadas*

a – Coconut Chutney; b – Onion Chutney; c – Sambhar; d – Rava Kesari; e – Vadas; f – Idlis; g – Upama; h – Utthapam made from *idli* batter.

Rava Kesari (Saffron Semolina Dessert)

(see p. 28 d)

PREPARATION TIME: 5 MINUTES
COOKING TIME: 15 MINUTES
SERVES 4

1 cup semolina (*rava, suji*)

1/2 cup ghee
3 cups water
a few drops yellow food colour
a pinch saffron (*kesar*)
3/4 cup sugar
1 tbsp raisins
8 cashew nuts, chopped, fried

1. Heat the ghee in a pan, add the semolina and sauté until it turns pale gold and smells fragrant
2. Add the water, food colour and saffron; cook till the water is almost fully absorbed.
3. Add the sugar, raisins and cashew nuts, cook until the liquid released by the sugar is absorbed and the semolina is fluffed and moist; turn off the heat; keep the pan covered for 2 minutes; serve hot.

Malpuas (Rich Sweet Pancakes)

(see p. 39 g)

PREPARATION TIME: 20 MINUTES
COOKING TIME: 1 HOUR
SERVES 4

For the syrup:
$1\frac{1}{2}$ cups sugar
$1\frac{1}{2}$ cups water

For the rabri:
1 litre full cream milk
$\frac{1}{2}$ cup sugar
a pinch of saffron soaked in 1 tbsp milk

For the puas:
250 g flour
2 tbsp ghee
2 tbsp sugar
500 g full cream milk
1 tbsp aniseed (*saunf*)
2 tbsp mixed nuts, finely chopped
1 tbsp raisins
oil to shallow-fry
1 tbsp pistachios, chopped, to garnish

1. Put the sugar and water in a pan and boil for 10 minutes on low heat to make a syrup; reserve.
2. Boil the milk, stirring, until it is reduced to one-third; stir in the sugar and saffron and cook until the *rabri* is thick.
3. Put the flour, ghee and sugar in a bowl and mix together; gradually stir in the milk and blend to make a smooth batter; add the aniseed, chopped nuts and raisins.
4. Heat the oil in a frying pan; drop 2 to 3 tbsp of batter and spread it into a pancake about $6\frac{1}{2}$ cm ($2\frac{1}{2}$") in diameter; fry on both sides on low heat till golden; remove and drain. Make all the pancakes in this manner. Note that if the batter breaks up in the oil add a little more flour to it; if the pancake is too thick add more milk to the batter.
5. Soak the pancakes in syrup for 2 minutes; remove and drain; arrange on a flat serving dish; pour the *rabri* over the pancakes and garnish with pistachios.

COOK'S NOTE
Mixed nuts could include coconut, dates, almonds and cashews.

Dahi Bhallas with Tamarind Chutney (Yogurt Delight)

(see p. 39 b)

PREPARATION TIME: 40 MINUTES
SOAKING TIME: 4 – 6 HOURS
COOKING TIME: 30 MINUTES
SERVES 4

For the bhallas:
250 g split black gram (*dhuli safed urad* dal)
1″ ginger, thinly slivered
1 tbsp raisins
1 tbsp melon seeds (*magaz*)
oil to deep-fry

For the yogurt:
500 g yogurt
water as required
1/2 tsp red chilli powder
1 tsp dry-roasted cumin powder (see p. 12)
1/2 tsp black salt
salt to taste
1 tsp sugar

tamarind chutney to serve (see p. 12)

1. Soak the dal for 4 to 6 hours; drain; place in a blender and grind to make a fine paste; add a spoonful of water and beat the paste for 5 to 10 minutes or till it becomes light but remains quite thick. Drop a tsp of the batter into a bowl of water – if it floats, it is ready. Stir the ginger, raisins and melon seeds into the batter.
2. Shape about 2 tbsp of batter into a patty, *bhalla*, using wet fingers to prevent sticking.
3. Heat the oil in a wok, *karhai*, add the *bhallas* and fry them on medium heat in batches till golden brown; remove and drain; soak the *bhallas* for 15 to 20 minutes in a bowl of warm, salted water; remove, squeeze gently to remove excess water and arrange in a shallow serving dish.
4. Whisk the yogurt along with the rest of the ingredients; pour over the *bhallas*; dribble tamarind chutney over the top, or serve separately; serve cold.

Sweet and Sour Pumpkin

(see p. 39 c)

PREPARATION TIME: 15 MINUTES
COOKING TIME: 40 MINUTES
SERVES 4

1 kg pumpkin (*kaddu*)

3 tbsp oil
1/2 tsp fenugreek seeds (*methi dana*)
1/2 tsp cumin seeds
1/2 tsp onion seeds (*kalonji*)
2 dry red chillies
1 tsp aniseed (*saunf*)
1″ ginger, finely diced
1 tsp turmeric powder
1 tsp red chilli powder
1 tsp garam masala powder
salt to taste
3 tbsp sugar
1 tbsp dried mango powder (*amchur*)

1. Cut the pumpkin into small cubes, leaving the skin on.
2. Heat the oil in a pan and temper it with the fenugreek, cumin and onion seeds along with the red chillies and aniseed, adding them one by one; add the ginger and sauté until it turns golden.
3. Stir in the pumpkin; sprinkle with turmeric, red chilli and garam masala powders and salt; cover and cook on low heat until the pumpkin is tender.
4. Stir in the sugar and dried mango powder and cook on high heat till any liquid that remains in the pan evaporates; serve hot with puris.

COOK'S NOTE

- Sugar brings out the natural sweetness of pumpkin. Served with puris, it is one of the all-time favourites on a vegetarian menu.
- If the skin of the pumpkin is soft it may be left on; otherwise it should be removed.

Dal Kachoris (Stuffed Bread)

PREPARATION TIME: 40 MINUTES
SOAKING TIME: 5 – 6 HOURS
COOKING TIME: 20 MINUTES
SERVES 4

For the stuffing:
200 g skinless black gram (*dhuli safed urad* dal)
2 tbsp oil
1 tsp cumin seeds
a pinch asafoetida (*hing*)
1/2 tsp red chilli powder
1 tbsp coriander powder
1/2 tsp garam masala powder
1 tbsp aniseed (*saunf*)
1 tsp ginger paste
salt to taste

For the dough:
1/2 kg wholewheat flour (*ata*)
1 tbsp oil
1 tsp carom seeds (*ajwain*)
salt to taste
water as required

1. Soak the *urad* dal for 5 to 6 hours; drain; put in a blender and grind to fine paste.
2. Heat the oil in a pan, add the cumin seeds and asafoetida; when the cumin seeds begin to brown stir in the dal paste; add the red chilli, coriander and garam masala powders, aniseed, ginger paste and salt; sauté the dal until the water evaporates; cool.
3. Sift the flour into a bowl, add the oil, carom seeds, salt and water and knead to make a soft dough; divide the dough into walnut-sized balls. Flatten a ball of dough, place 1 tbsp of the filling in the centre, close a shape into a ball again; roll out the ball into a circle 10 cm (4") in diameter, using a little oil to prevent sticking.
4. Heat the oil in a wok, *karhai,* and fry the *kachoris* one at a time until golden brown; drain; serve hot with Raseydar Alu (see p. 37).

Raseydar Alu (Gravied Potatoes)

PREPARATION TIME: 20 MINUTES
COOKING TIME: 30 – 40 MINUTES
SERVES 4

1 kg potatoes, boiled, cubed

4 tbsp oil
1 tsp fenugreek seeds (*methi dana*)
1 tsp cumin seeds
2 dry red chillies
1 bay leaf
2 black cardamoms (*badi elaichi*)
5-6 peppercorns
3-4 cloves
1″ cinnamon
1″ ginger, finely chopped
2 green chillies, sliced
2 tsp turmeric powder
1 tsp red chilli powder
1 tbsp coriander powder
salt to taste
4 medium tomatoes, blanched, peeled, chopped
3/4 cup yogurt, whisked
water as required
1 tbsp coriander leaves, chopped, to garnish

1. Heat the oil in a pan, add the fenugreek and cumin seeds, dry red chillies, bay leaf, black cardamoms, peppercorns, cloves and cinnamon and fry till fragrant; add the ginger, green chillies, turmeric, red chilli and coriander powders and salt; stir for 30 to 40 seconds.
2. Add the tomatoes and cook till the oil comes to the surface. Add the potatoes then add the yogurt, a little at a time to prevent curdling, and sauté for 5 minutes on low heat. Crush some potatoes to thicken the gravy, adding water as required; cover and simmer for 10 to 15 minutes; garnish with coriander leaves and serve with *kachoris* (see p. 34).

COOK'S NOTE
A popular accompaniment for a north Indian *thali* is *Mooli Lachcha*: Grate 2 large radishes and squeeze out the water; mix in 1-2 tbsp finely slivered ginger, 1-2 tbsp finely chopped green chillies, 2 tbsp pomegranates, 2 tbsp lemon juice and salt to taste.

Accompaniments for a north Indian Thali

Mango Pickle

PREPARATION TIME: 6 HOURS
MATURATION TIME: 7 – 10 DAYS

1 kg raw green mangoes
4 tbsp salt
200 ml oil, preferably mustard oil
1½ tbsp turmeric powder
1 tbsp red chilli powder
1 tbsp mustard (*rai*) powder
1 tbsp fenugreek seeds (*methi*)
1 tsp onion seeds (*kalonji*)
2 tbsp aniseed (*saunf*), coarsely powdered
2 tbsp vinegar

Wash the mangoes and wipe dry; cut into small pieces, with skin, and discard the pits. Rub 2 tbsp of the salt into the mangoes and keep aside for 2 to 3 hours. Drain the water that comes out of the mangoes and dry them in the sun for 2 to 3 hours. Warm the oil in a pan, add the turmeric, red chilli and mustard powders, fenugreek and onion seeds, aniseed, the rest of the salt and the mangoes; mix thoroughly; transfer to a glass jar; pour the vinegar into the jar and close the lid tightly. Keep the jar in the sun for 7 to 10 days – the pickle is ready to use.

Sweet-Sour Mango Chutney

PREPARATION TIME: 20 MINUTES
COOKING TIME: 1 HOUR

1 kg raw green mangoes
1 kg sugar
1 tbsp fenugreek seeds (*methi dana*)
1 tbsp onion seeds (*kalonji*)
1 tbsp garam masala powder
1 tsp red chilli powder
1 tbsp aniseed (*saunf*)
2 tbsp salt
1 tbsp vinegar

Wash and peel the mangoes and chop them finely, discarding the pits; place in a pan along with the rest of the ingredients except the vinegar and cook on medium heat until the mixture looks like jam; remove the pan from the stove, cool then add the vinegar; transfer to a glass jar – the chutney is ready to eat.

a – Pulao with Peas; b – Dahi Bhallas; c – Sweet and sour Pumpkin; d – Raseydar Alu; e – Sweet-Sour Mango Chutney; f – Mango Pickle; g – Malpuas; h – Mooli Lachcha; i – Dal Kachoris.

a
b
c
d
e
f
g
h
i

Alu Parathas with Lassi

PREPARATION TIME: 20 MINUTES
COOKING TIME: 20 MINUTES
SERVES 4

For the stuffing:
4 medium potatoes, boiled, mashed
2 medium onions, finely chopped
1/2 tsp red chilli powder
1/2 tsp garam masala powder
2 green chillies, chopped
1 tbsp coriander leaves, chopped
salt to taste

2 cups wholewheat flour (*ata*)
water as required
oil to shallow-fry

1. Put the potatoes in a bowl along with the onions, red chilli and garam masala powders, green chillies, coriander leaves and salt and mix together; divide into 8 portions.
2. Put the flour and water in a bowl; knead to make a soft, pliable dough; divide the dough into 8 equal portions and make smooth balls. Roll out a ball of dough and place the stuffing in the centre; bring the edges of the dough together and close it; carefully roll out a paratha approximately 15 cm (6") in diameter.
3. Heat a griddle, *tawa*, and place a paratha on it; cook on low heat till spots appear on one side; turn and cook the other side, dribbling a little oil around the edges; cook until golden brown on both sides.

Salty Lassi: Put 2 cups fresh yogurt, 2 tsp salt, 1 tsp dry-roasted cumin powder, 2 cups cold water, 1 cup ice cubes in a blender; blend for 2 minutes; pour the lassi into tall glasses; serve chilled.

Sweet Lassi: Omit the salt and cumin powder; add 6 tbsp sugar and reduce the water to half.

Mango Lassi: Add 1 cup mango pulp to Sweet Lassi and reduce the sugar; add a pinch of cardamom powder and a pinch of saffron

Besan Pudas (Gram Flour Pancakes)

PREPARATION TIME: 20 MINUTES
COOKING TIME: 20 MINUTES
SERVES 4

For the filling:
2 tbsp oil
1 large onion, finely diced
2 green chillies, finely chopped
1/2" ginger, chopped
100 g green peas, shelled
250 g cottage cheese (paneer), crumbled
1/2 tsp garam masala powder
salt to taste

For the pudas:
250 g gram flour (*besan*)
1 tsp carom seeds (*ajwain*)
salt to taste
water as required

oil to shallow-fry

1. Heat the oil in a pan, add the onions, green chillies and ginger and sau until the onions turn pale gold; add the peas and cook, covered, until tender; stir in the paneer, garam masala powder and salt; sauté until th mixture becomes dry; remove and cool.
2. Put the gram flour in a bowl along with the carom seeds and salt; add water to make a batter suitable for pancakes; beat until smooth.
3. Heat a griddle, *tawa*, pour 2 tbsp batter on it and spread to make a th pancake; dribble oil around the edges; turn and cook the other side. Pl 2 tbsp of the filling in the centre and fold the pancake over it; serve ho with mint-coriander chutney (see p. 12).

high tea

Fish Cutlets

PREPARATION TIME: 10 MINUTES
COOKING TIME: 30 MINUTES
SERVES 4

1/2 kg boneless fish, diced

1/2 tsp salt
1 small onion, chopped
2 green chillies, chopped
1 tbsp coriander leaves, chopped
1/2 tsp red chilli powder
1 tsp garam masala powder
2 slices bread, crumbled
oil to deep-fry

mint-coriander chutney, to serve (see p. 12)

1. Put the fish in a non-stick pan and cook on low heat, covered, for about 5 minutes or until it becomes tender; transfer to a bowl and mash the fish with a wooden spoon.
2. Add the salt, onions, green chillies, coriander leaves, red chilli and garam masala powders and bread and mix well; divide into cutlets approximately 5 cm (2″) in diameter and 1 cm (1/2″) thick.
3. Heat the oil in a pan and fry the cutlets until golden brown; serve hot with mint-coriander chutney.

Sandwiches

PREPARATION TIME: 10 – 30 MINUTES
SERVES 4

For the tuna filling:
100 g tuna, canned
3 tbsp fresh herbs, chopped
3 tbsp mayonnaise
1 tsp Dijon mustard
salt and pepper to taste

Combine all the ingredients, season with salt and pepper to taste.

For the green chutney filling:
10 cashew nuts, soaked in water, drained
1/2 cup raisins, soaked in water, drained
1 1/2 cups coriander leaves, chopped
1 1/2 tsp lemon juice
salt to taste

Put all the ingredients in a blender and grind to made a fine paste.

For the yogurt filling:
1 cup drained yogurt (see p. 12)
salt and pepper to taste
sliced tomatoes and cucumbers

For the sandwiches:
8 slices firm sandwich bread
lettuce to garnish

Spread the filling of your choice generously on four slices of bread; if the yogurt filling is used lay the tomato or cucumber slices over it; cover the filling with the remaining slices of bread; cut off the crusts with a sharp knife and cut into triangles; serve on a bed of lettuce.

Samosas

PREPARATION TIME: 30 MINUTES
COOKING TIME: 30 MINUTES
SERVES 4

For the filling:
2 tbsp oil
1" ginger, finely chopped
1 green chilli, chopped
1 tsp cumin seeds
250 g peas, shelled
1/2 tsp red chilli powder
1/2 tsp garam masala powder
salt to taste
1/2 kg potatoes, boiled, finely diced

200 g flour
1 tbsp oil
1 tsp carom seeds (*ajwain*)
salt to taste
water as required
oil to deep-fry
mint-coriander chutney, to serve (see p. 12)

1. Heat the oil in a pan, add the ginger, green chilli and cumin seeds and fry till fragrant; stir in the peas, sprinkle with the red chilli and garam masala powders and salt, cover and cook till tender. Stir in the potatoes and cook for 2 to 3 minutes; cool.
2. Put the flour in a bowl and stir in the oil, carom seeds, salt and water; knead to make a medium-soft dough; divide into 10 smooth balls.
3. Roll a ball of dough into a circle, about 15 cm (6") in diameter; cut the circle into two equal halves, using a sharp knife. Shape one half into a cone, wet the edges and seal; put some potato filling into the cone and seal the samosa to close it, wetting the edges.
4. Heat the oil in a wok, *karhai*, add a few samosas at a time and deep-fry on medium heat until golden brown and crisp; remove with a slotted spoon; drain; serve hot with mint-coriander chutney.

COOK'S NOTE

- For cocktail-sized samosas make the cones smaller to get 16 from the given recipe.
- For a non-vegetarian version, use a filling of cooked minced mutton.
- To freeze samosas, half-fry and remove before the dough changes colour; cool and freeze in airtight containers. To serve, thaw for 2 hours; deep-fry in hot oil until golden brown.

Fruit Chaat (Spicy Fruit Salad)

PREPARATION TIME: 30 MINUTES
COOKING TIME: 15 MINUTES
SERVES 4

2 large potatoes, parboiled
oil to shallow-fry
1 orange
250 g papaya, peeled, deseeded, diced
1 guava, deseeded, diced
1 apple, diced
1 nectarine, diced
2 bananas, peeled, thickly sliced
1/2 cup pomegranate
10-15 black grapes

1 tbsp chaat masala (commercially available)
1 tbsp lemon juice
1 tbsp tamarind chutney (see p. 12), to serve
1 tbsp mint-coriander chutney (see p. 12), to serve

1. Peel the potatoes, cut into 1" cubes and shallow-fry until golden brown on all sides and cooked through to the centre; remove and drain thoroughly; place them in a large bowl.
2. Peel the orange and remove the membrane around the segments; add t the bowl along with the papaya, guava, apple, nectarine, bananas, pomegranate and grapes.
3. Stir the chaat masala and lemon juice into the fruit chaat. Serve with tamarind chutney and mint-coriander chutney, which may be spooned into the bowl, or dribbled over the top of individual servings to taste, fo an extra sharp and tangy flavour.

Instant Dhoklas (Steamed Savoury Squares)

PREPARATION TIME: 20 MINUTES
COOKING TIME: 30 MINUTES
SERVES 4

For the dhoklas:
1 cup gram flour (*besan*)
1 tbsp oil
1 tsp ginger paste
1 tsp green chilli paste
1/2 tsp turmeric powder
1 tsp sugar
salt to taste
1 tsp lemon juice
1 1/4 cups yogurt
water as required
1 tsp Eno fruit salt (commercially available)

Tempering:
1 tbsp oil
1 tsp mustard seeds (*sarson*)
1 tsp sesame seeds (*til*)
3-4 green chillies, slit lengthwise
1 tbsp vinegar
1 tbsp sugar
1/2 cup water

coriander leaves, chopped, to garnish
grated coconut, chopped, to garnish

1. Put the gram flour in a bowl and stir in the oil, ginger paste, green chilli paste, turmeric powder, sugar, salt, lemon juice and yogurt; add water as required to make a batter, the consistency of thick sauce.
2. Fill a steamer with water and bring it to a boil; grease a dish approximately 15 1/2 cm square and 5 cm high (6 x 6 x 2") and place it over the steamer; stir the Eno fruit salt into the batter and immediately pour it into the dish; steam for 15 minutes or until the mixture is firm; remove and cool.
3. Transfer the *dhokla* to a serving platter by inverting the dish over it; cut into squares.
4. Heat the oil in a pan, add the mustard seeds and when they start to splutter add the sesame seeds and green chillies; cool a little then carefully add the vinegar, sugar and water; bring to a boil, cook for 2 minutes then pour over the *dhokla* and leave for 20 minutes to get absorbed. Garnish with coriander leaves and coconut.

Brownies

PREPARATION TIME: 15 MINUTES
BAKING TIME: 20 MINUTES
SERVES 4

60 g cocoa
230 g sugar
75 g butter, at room temperature
2 eggs
180 g flour
1/2 tsp baking powder
3/4 cup walnuts, coarsely chopped

a square cake tin, 21 x 21cm (8 x 8"), greased

1. Put the cocoa, sugar and butter in a bowl and beat for 2 minutes; beat in the eggs, one at a time, to make a smooth batter.
2. Sift the flour and baking powder together; stir into the batter; transfer the batter to the cake tin and even the surface; cover with the walnuts; bake for 20 minutes or until the surface becomes shiny but firm. Cut into squares and serve.

Carefree Cheesecake

PREPARATION TIME: 30 MINUTES
CHILLING TIME: 2 – 4 HOURS
SERVES 4

For the biscuit base:
1 cup wholewheat biscuit crumbs
100 g butter, at room temperature
a 23 cm (9") spring-form cake tin

For the filling:
1 cup water
1 tbsp unflavoured gelatine
1/2 cup sugar
250 g cream cheese
1 tsp vanilla essence
a few slices of kiwi, strawberries, or any other fruit

1. Put the biscuit crumbs and butter in a bowl and mix till well blended; press evenly into the base of the cake tin; chill the biscuit base in the refrigerator for 15 minutes.
2. Put the water, gelatine and sugar in a pan; hold the pan over a larger pan of simmering water; stir until the gelatine and sugar are fully dissolved; cool to room temperature.
3. Put the cream cheese, vanilla essence and the gelatine-sugar mixture in a blender and blend till smooth; pour over the biscuit base; chill in the refrigerator for 2 to 4 hours or until it sets.
4. Remove the spring to open the cake tin and slide the cheesecake onto a serving platter. Garnish with the fresh fruit slices.

COOK'S NOTE

- A spring-form cake tin is always round; the side unclips, allowing the base, with the dessert on it, to be lifted out without breaking.
- Cream cheese is the key ingredient in a cheesecake. It is a smooth and spreadable cheese, usually sold in blocks; a popular brand is Philadelphia Cream Cheese.

Marble Cake

PREPARATION TIME: 20 MINUTES
BAKING TIME: 40 MINUTES
SERVES 4

4 eggs
1 cup sugar
1 tsp vanilla essence
3/4 cup oil/melted butter
1 cup flour
2 tsp baking powder
1 tbsp cocoa

a 23 cm (9") ring-shaped cake tin, greased, floured

1. Put the eggs and sugar in a bowl and beat till pale and fluffy; add the vanilla essence and oil/butter and stir to mix the batter.
2. Sift the flour and baking powder together, then fold into the batter; pour two-third of the batter into the ring-shaped tin; mix the cocoa into the remaining batter and pour it into the tin; bake the cake in a preheated oven, 180C/350F, for 40 minutes or until the top is shiny but firm and the cake leaves the sides of the pan; or insert a skewer/cake tester into the cake and if it comes out clean the cake is ready; remove from the oven and allow to cool; invert onto a serving platter.

Quick Chocolate Cake

PREPARATION TIME: 15 MINUTES
BAKING TIME: 25 MINUTES
SERVES 4

2 tbsp cocoa

1/4 cup corn oil
1/2 cup water
3 eggs
150 g sugar
1 tsp vanilla essence
120 g flour
2 tsp baking powder
a pinch of salt
a loaf-shaped cake tin,
26 x 10 x 8 cm (10 x 4 x 3")

For the icing:
3 squares unsweetened chocolate
3 tbsp butter
1 1/2 cups confectioners' sugar
1/2 cup milk or water, boiling hot

1. Put the cocoa, oil and water in a pan and boil for two minutes; remove the pan from the stove and keep aside.
2. Put the eggs, sugar and essence in a bowl and beat until pale and fluffy.
3. Sift the flour, baking powder and salt; stir into the egg mixture along with the reserved cocoa liquid, pour the batter into the cake tin and bake in a preheated oven at 180C/350F for 25 minutes, or until a cake-tester inserted in the middle comes out clean. Allow to cool; invert onto a serving platter.
4. Put the chocolate and butter in a pan and place over low heat until the chocolate melts; remove the pan from the stove, stir in the sugar, add the milk/water and beat until smooth; while still warm, spread the icing over the cake. Use a cake comb to create wavy lines over the surface.

Trifle Pudding

PREPARATION TIME: 30 MINUTES
COOKING TIME: 10 MINUTES
SERVES 4

a 23 cm (9") round sponge cake, 4 cm ($1^1/_2$") thick

1 cup strawberry jelly
2 cups vanilla custard sauce (commercially available)
$1^1/_2$ cups orange juice
2 tsp sherry or liqueur (optional)
$1^1/_2$ cups mixed fresh fruit, diced
1 cup cream, whipped
1 kiwi, peeled and sliced
8-10 strawberries, halved
8-10 black grapes, halved

1. Prepare the jelly and the custard sauce according to the instructions on their respective packets.
2. Slice the sponge cake horizontally into three layers.
3. Line the bottom of a glass serving bowl with a layer of sponge cake and sprinkle with $^1/_2$ cup orange juice and some sherry/liqueur. Cover with one-third of the fresh fruit, one-third of the jelly and one-third of the custard; repeat the layers.
4. Decorate the top with the cream and garnish with kiwi, strawberries and grapes.

Steamed Bread Pudding

PREPARATION TIME: 20 MINUTES
COOKING TIME: 20 MINUTES
SERVES 4

2 slices white bread

3 tbsp desiccated coconut
$1\frac{1}{2}$ cups milk, boiled
3 eggs
1 tin sweetened condensed milk
1 tsp vanilla essence
1 cup cream, whipped, to garnish
6 red cherries, to garnish

a 21 cm (8") round cake tin

1. Put the bread and coconut in a bowl, add the milk and soak for 10 minutes; transfer to a blender; add the eggs, condensed milk and vanilla essence and blend for 5 minutes at medium speed.
2. Pour the mixture into the cake tin, cover with foil, place over a large pan of simmering water and steam for 20 minutes; remove and cool; invert onto a serving platter and chill; garnish with the cream and cherries.

Date Pudding

PREPARATION TIME: 30 MINUTES
BAKING TIME: 45 MINUTES
SERVES 4

2 cups dates, chopped

1 cup boiling water
1 cup all-purpose flour
3/4 tsp baking soda
1/2 cup walnuts, chopped
3 tbsp butter, melted
1 1/2 cups brown sugar, firmly packed
1 egg
1 cup cream
a 21 cm (8") square cake tin, greased

1. Place the dates in a bowl and cover with the water; set aside till cool.
2. Sift the flour and baking soda together; stir in the walnuts.
3. Put the butter and brown sugar in a bowl and beat well; beat in the egg; fold in the flour mixture then the date mixture; pour the batter into the cake tin and bake at 180C/350F for 40 to 45 minutes or until the top springs back when lightly pressed in the centre. Serve warm with cream.

Hot Fruit Crumble

PREPARATION TIME: 20 MINUTES
BAKING TIME: 50 MINUTES
SERVES 4

1 kg apples, peeled, cored, sliced
100 g sugar

***For the crumble*:**
100 g butter
200 g flour
50 g castor sugar

1. Arrange the apples in layers in a deep, glass ovenproof dish, sprinkling the sugar between the layers.
2. Rub the butter into the flour till it resembles fine breadcrumbs; stir in the castor sugar.
3. Sprinkle the crumble over the apples, without pressing it down as this will make it heavy.
4. Bake for approximately 45 minutes in a preheated oven at 180C/350F, or until crisp and golden on top. Serve hot with cream or vanilla ice cream.

COOK'S NOTE
Pears, apricots, peaches or plums may be used in place of apples.

Tiramisu

PREPARATION TIME: 45 MINUTES
CHILLING TIME: 1 HOUR
SERVES 4

1 packet sponge fingers or sponge cake cut into fingers

2 eggs
4 tbsp castor sugar
250 g mascarpone cheese
300 ml cream, whipped
125 ml hot, strong, black coffee
2 tbsp amaretto or brandy
50 g dark chocolate, grated
cocoa to garnish

1. Whisk the eggs and sugar in a bowl until thick and fluffy.
2. Lightly beat the mascarpone cheese in a bowl, fold in the egg mixture and the cream.
3. Mix the coffee with amaretto in a shallow dish.
4. Dip the sponge fingers in the coffee and lay them in the base of a glass serving dish; cover with half the mascarpone-cream mixture and half the grated chocolate; repeat the layers; chill the pudding in the refrigerator for 1 hour; before serving, lightly sift cocoa through a wire sieve over the top.

COOK'S NOTE

- In Italian tiramisu mean 'pick me up'; this traditional dessert has many variations.
- Mascarpone is a rich, creamy, soft cheese from Italy with a very high proportion of fat. There is no good substitute for mascarpone but in an emergency mix equal quantities of cream cheese and sour cream; or blend ricotta cheese with heavy cream in a blender.

Butter Cookies

PREPARATION TIME: 15 MINUTES
CHILLING TIME: 30 – 60 MINUTES
BAKING TIME: 10 MINUTES
SERVES 4

60 g butter, softened

120 g castor sugar
150 g flour
1/2 tsp vanilla essence

a baking tray

1. Put the butter and sugar in a bowl and beat with a wooden spoon till smooth and light; stir in the flour and vanilla essence; chill in the refrigerator for about 1 hour.
2. Spread a sheet of butter paper on a kitchen table and roll out the dough; cut the dough into shapes with a cookie cutter. Arrange on a greased baking tray.
3. Bake for 8 to 10 minutes in a preheated oven at 180C/350F. Remove and cool on a wire rack.

Chocolate Mousse

PREPARATION TIME: 10 MINUTES
COOKING TIME: 20 MINUTES
CHILLING TIME: 1 – 2 HOURS
SERVES 4

- 1/2 cup cold water
- 1 envelope unflavoured gelatine
- 1/2 cup cottage cheese
- 1/2 cup cream
- 1/3 cup sugar
- 3 tbsp unsweetened cocoa
- 1 cup milk
- 1 tsp vanilla essence

1. Put the water in a small pan, stir in the gelatine and let it stand for 5 minutes; hold the pan over a larger pan of simmering water and stir until the gelatine dissolves; keep aside.
2. Put the cottage cheese in a blender along with the cream, sugar and cocoa; add 2-3 tbsp of milk and blend till smooth; gradually add the rest of the milk; add the vanilla essence and the warm gelatine and blend well. Pour the mixture into a serving bowl, chill, stirring occasionally; chill for 1 to 2 hours or until thick and creamy.

COOK'S NOTE

Gelatine is an odourless, tasteless and colourless thickening agent which, when dissolved and cooled, forms a jelly. Soak gelati in cold water to soften it; dissolve it over simmering water since it gets damaged by direct heat. Traditional gelatine is an anim product but vegetarian forms are also available. It is sold in a granular form in standard-size sachets (envelopes) of 7 g (1/4 oz

Apple Pie

PREPARATION TIME: 30 MINUTES
BAKING TIME: 40 MINUTES
SERVES 4

For the base:
2 cups flour
a pinch of salt
3/4 cup butter, chilled
1/2 cup cold water

For the filling:
5 green apples, thinly sliced
1 tsp cinnamon powder
3/4 cup brown sugar
2 tbsp almonds, chopped

For the egg glaze:
1 egg yolk beaten with 1 tbsp milk

a 23 cm (9") ovenproof pie dish
vanilla ice cream, to serve

1. Put the flour and salt in a bowl and rub in the butter; add the cold water and knead to make a dough; divide the dough into 2 unequal portions.
2. Roll out the larger portion on a lightly floured surface and line the base of the pie dish; refrigerate for 10 minutes.
3. Mix the apples, cinnamon and brown sugar in a bowl; spread them in a layer in the pie dish; sprinkle the almonds on top.
4. Roll out the remaining dough, place it over the apples and press the edges together; prick it with a fork to make a design and to let steam escape.
5. Bake in a preheated oven at 200C/400F for 20 to 25 minutes; remove and brush the top with the egg glaze; put back in the oven and bake for another 15 minutes or until golden. Serve warm with vanilla ice cream.

cocktails

Fish Fingers

PREPARATION TIME: 15 MINUTES
COOKING TIME: 20 MINUTES
SERVES 4

250 g fish fillets, cut into fingers

2 tbsp lemon juice
1 tsp salt
3 tbsp dry breadcrumbs
oil to deep-fry

1. Rub the fish fingers with lemon juice and salt and marinate for 10 minutes.
2. Spread the breadcrumbs on a tray; roll the fish fingers in them to get well coated.
3. Heat the oil in a pan and deep-fry the fish fingers in batches until golden brown; drain; serve hot with tomato or chilli sauce.

Seekh Kebabs

PREPARATION TIME: 20 MINUTES
MARINATING TIME: 2 HOURS
COOKING TIME: 10 MINUTES
SERVES 4

$^{1}/_{2}$ kg fat-free mutton, ground

For the masala paste:
2 onions, chopped
8 cloves garlic
$^{1}/_{2}$" ginger
2 tbsp coriander leaves, chopped
1 tbsp mint leaves, chopped
5 green chillies, chopped
1 tsp red chilli powder
1 tsp coriander powder
2 tsp garam masala powder
4 black cardamoms (*badi elaichi*), powdered
1 tsp lemon juice
salt to taste

6 rods or skewers for grilling

1. Put all the ingredients for the masala paste into a blender and grind till smooth; rub the paste thoroughly into the ground meat; keep aside for hours.
2. Divide the ground meat into 6 equal portions. Mould each portion around a skewer to make 10 cm (4") long kebabs, wetting your fingers to prevent sticking.
3. Cook the kebabs over a hot barbeque, rotating the skewers gently, for 4 to 6 minutes or until tender and golden. Alternatively, place the skewers in a hot oven and bake for 8 to 10 minutes.
4. Remove the kebabs from the skewers, cut in half and serve with mint-coriander chutney (see p. 12).

Vegetable Pakoras

PREPARATION TIME: 20 MINUTES
COOKING TIME: 30 MINUTES
SERVES 4

2 medium potatoes, peeled
8-10 cauliflower florets
2 medium onions
8-10 spinach leaves

For the batter:
250 g gram flour (*besan*)
1 tsp carom seeds (*ajwain*)
2 green chillies, finely chopped
2 tbsp coriander leaves, finely chopped
2 tsp salt
water as required

oil to deep-fry
chaat masala (commercially available)

1. Peel and thinly slice the potatoes; cut the cauliflower into $2\frac{1}{2}$ cm (1") florets; thinly slice the onions, without separating the rings; keep the spinach leaves whole.
2. Put the gram flour in a bowl, add the carom seeds, green chillies, coriander leaves, salt and water and mix to make a smooth batter of coating consistency.
3. Heat the oil in a wok, *karhai*. Dip the vegetables in the batter one by one and drop them into the oil. Fry in batches on medium heat till the outside is golden and the inside is cooked through. If the oil is too hot the outside will get browned while the inside will remain raw; remove with a slotted spoon; drain.
4. Arrange the pakoras on a platter and sprinkle chaat masala over them; serve hot with any chutney.

Malai Chicken Tikkas

PREPARATION TIME: 10 MINUTES
MARINATING TIME: 4 – 5 HOURS
COOKING TIME: 15 MINUTES
SERVES 4

6 chicken breasts, skinless, boneless

For the first marinade:
3 tsp ginger paste
3 tsp garlic paste
1 tsp white pepper powder
2 tsp salt

For the second marinade:
1 egg
3/4 cup cream
2 tbsp cashew nut paste
4 green chillies, chopped
2 tbsp coriander leaves, chopped
1 tsp cardamom powder
2 tbsp cornflour

butter for basting
rods or skewers for grilling

1. Clean and cut the chicken breasts into 4 pieces; rub the ginger and garli pastes, white pepper and salt into the chicken and keep aside for 15 minutes.
2. Whisk the egg in a bowl; stir in the rest of the ingredients for the marinade, add the chicken and marinate for 4 hours.
3. Skewer the chicken pieces onto the rods, 2½ cm (1") apart; grill in a preheated oven for 6 minutes, basting with butter; remove the rods, stand upright and allow them to drip; grill again for 3 minutes or until tender and well done. Serve hot with mint-coriander chutney (see p. 12

Paneer Tikkas

PREPARATION TIME: 10 MINUTES
MARINATING TIME: 30 MINUTES
COOKING TIME: 15 MINUTES
SERVES 4

500 g cottage cheese (paneer)

1 green bell pepper (capsicum) (*simla mirch*)
1 red bell pepper
1 yellow bell pepper
2 large onions

For the marinade:
1/4 cup yogurt
1/4 cup tomato purée
1 tsp garam masala powder
1 tsp tandoori masala (commercially available)
a pinch tandoori food colour
salt to taste

rods or skewers for grilling

1. Cut the paneer, all the bell peppers and the onions into $2\frac{1}{2}$ cm (1″) cubes and put them in a bowl.
2. Mix all the ingredients for the marinade and pour into the bowl; stir till the paneer and vegetables are well coated; marinate for 30 minutes.
3. Skewer the paneer, bell peppers and onions alternately in a decorative manner and arrange the skewers in an oven tray; place the tray in a preheated oven and bake at 180C/350F for 15 minutes, rotating the skewers so that the tikkas become evenly browned. Alternately, grill or barbecue the skewers; or place them in a greased frying pan and cook till well done.

COOK'S NOTE
If bamboo skewers are used they should be presoaked for 1 hour.

Khandvis (Steamed Rolls)

PREPARATION TIME: 10 MINUTES
COOKING TIME: 15 MINUTES
SERVES 4

For the khandvis:
1 cup gram flour (*besan*)
salt to taste
$^{1}/_{2}$ tsp turmeric powder
3 cups buttermilk
OR
1 cup yogurt and 2 cups water

Tempering:
1 tbsp oil
1 tsp mustard seeds
2 dry red chillies, halved

grated coconut, to garnish
coriander leaves, to garnish

1. Mix all the ingredients and beat till smooth and free from lumps; transfer to a heatproof bowl.
2. Fill an inch or two of water in a pressure cooker and place the bowl inside, using a trivet if required so that the water level is well below the rim of the bowl; bring to pressure and cook for 2 minutes; remove the pan from the stove and allow the pressure to reduce completely before opening the lid.
3. Pour the hot batter onto a greased surface and spread it out into a very thin sheet, using a flat knife; cut it into $2^{1}/_{2}$ cm (1″) strips and carefully roll each strip tightly to form a roll. Arrange all the rolls, *khandvis,* in a serving dish.
4. Heat the oil in a small pan, temper the oil with the mustard seeds and red chillies and pour over the *khandvis*; garnish with coconut and coriander leaves; serve at room temperature.

Momos (Steamed Samosas)

PREPRATION TIME: 30 MINUTES
COOKING TIME: 15 MINUTES
SERVES 4

For the filling:
500 g boneless chicken, minced
250 g onions, finely chopped
2″ ginger, grated
salt to taste

For the dough:
400 g flour
water as required

For the chilli sauce:
10 dry red chillies
1″ ginger
1 tbsp peanuts, roasted
salt to taste

steamer stand with perforated baskets (see Cook's Note)

1. Mix all the ingredients for the filling and keep aside.
2. Put the flour in a bowl, add water and knead to make a stiff dough. Divide the dough into marble-sized balls, dip a ball in flour and roll it out into a thin circle. Dip your finger in water then trace it around the edge of the circle to wet it. To make semi-circular *momos*, place $1/2$ tsp filling on one half of the circle and fold the other half over it, pressing the edges together. Prepare all the *momos* in this manner; arrange them in the perforated steamer baskets.
3. Fill some water in the base of the steamer and bring it to a boil; insert the baskets with *momos* and steam for 10 minutes; transfer the bottom container to the top and steam for another 5 minutes or until the *momos* look shiny and the filling is cooked.
4. Boil the dry red chillies for a few minutes; drain; grind along with the ginger, peanuts and salt to make a smooth, thick chilli sauce to serve with the *momos*.

COOK'S NOTE

A traditional momo steamer, called a *matku*, has 4 sections: The base holds the water for steaming and the top three containers are perforated to allow the steam to circulate; a lid covers the top container. If a *matku* is not available you can improvise with a large pan and strainers or sieves to hold the *momos*.

Raw Vegetables with Dips

For the eggplant dip:
2 medium brinjals (aubergines, eggplants)
2 spring onions with 2″ greens
3 cloves garlic
3 tbsp olive oil
3 tbsp lemon juice
2 tbsp *tahini* (Middle Eastern sesame seed paste)
salt and pepper to taste

Bake the brinjals or roast them over a gas flame till the skin is charred and they are tender; peel and place in a food processor along with the rest of the ingredients; blend till smooth.

For the yogurt dip:
500 g yogurt, drained (see p. 12)
4 tbsp fresh herbs
1 tsp lemon rind, grated
1/2 tsp pepper, freshly ground
2 tbsp sour cream
salt to taste

The herbs could include parsley, dill and chives; mix everything together in a bowl and chill before serving.

The vegetables:
Carrots, cut into sticks
Cucumbers, cut into sticks
Broccoli, cut into florets
Cauliflower, cut into florets
Cherry tomatoes

Soak the carrots and cucumbers in iced water for 10 minutes; drain; arrange the vegetables in a circle on a serving platter; serve with dips.

For the walnut dip:
1 cup walnuts, chopped
2 tbsp fresh parsley
1/2 cup milk
1 clove garlic
1 cup feta cheese, crumbled
1 cup yogurt, drained (see p. 12)
salt to taste
2 tsp olive oil
1 tsp oregano

Put the walnuts and parsley in a blender and process for 2 minute; add the milk, garlic, feta cheese, yogurt and salt and blend to make a smooth dip; chill for 30 minutes; stir in the olive oil; transfer to a bowl and garnish with oregano.

Shami Kebabs

PREPARATION TIME: 1 HOUR
COOKING TIME: 20 MINUTES
SERVES 4

500 g boneless mutton, diced

1 medium onion, coarsely chopped
$^{1}/_{2}$ cup split Bengal gram (*chana* dal)
2″ cinnamon
4 cloves
4 cardamoms
2 tsp black cumin seeds (*shah jeera*)
salt to taste
1 tbsp oil
water as required
2 tbsp coriander leaves, chopped
2 tbsp mint, chopped
5 green chillies
$^{1}/_{2}$ cup yogurt

oil to shallow-fry

1. Wash and drain the meat; put it in a pan along with the onion, *chana* dal, cinnamon, cloves, cardamoms, black cumin seeds, salt, oil and water and boil until the meat and dal are tender. In a pressure cooker this will take 30 minutes. Sauté on high heat to evaporate any excess liquid in the pan; cool.
2. Grind the mixture along with the coriander leaves, mint and green chillies to make a fine paste; stir in the yogurt and divide the paste into small, round kebabs.
3. Heat the oil in a non-stick pan and shallow-fry 4 or 5 kebabs at a time till golden brown; turn and fry the other side; serve hot with mint-coriander chutney (see p. 12).

Spicy Meatballs

PREPARATION TIME: 10 MINUTES
COOKING TIME: 30 MINUTES
SERVES 4

For the meatballs:
1/2 kg boneless mutton/chicken, minced
1 large onion, finely chopped
2 green chillies, chopped
1 tbsp coriander leaves, chopped
2 tsp salt
1 tsp garam masala powder

oil to deep-fry

For the masala:
2 tbsp oil
3 tbsp onion paste
1/2 tsp red chilli powder
1 tsp salt
2-4 tbsp water

1. Put all the ingredients for the meatballs in a bowl and mix together; divide into walnut-sized balls.
2. Heat the oil in a wok, *karhai,* and deep-fry the meatballs on medium heat until golden brown; drain and reserve.
3. Heat the oil in a pan, add the onion paste and sauté till golden brown; stir in the red chilli powder and salt and sauté for 2 more minutes. Add the water and the meatballs, cover and simmer on low heat till the meatballs are well coated in the masala; serve hot.

Sesame Chicken Cubes

PREPARATION TIME: 30 MINUTES
MARINATING TIME: 1 HOUR 10 MINUTES
COOKING TIME: 20 MINUTES
SERVES 4

$^1/_2$ kg boneless chicken breast

***For the first marinade*:**
1 tbsp ginger paste
1 tbsp garlic paste
2 tbsp lemon juice
1 tsp yellow chilli powder (*peeli mirch*)
$^1/_2$ tsp white pepper powder

***For the second marinade*:**
$^1/_2$ cup yogurt, drained (see p. 12)
3 tbsp cream
$^1/_2$ tsp cardamom powder
$1^1/_2$ tbsp gram flour (*besan*)

1 cup breadcrumbs
$^1/_2$ cup sesame seeds (*til*)
oil to deep-fry

1. Wash and cut the chicken breasts into 4 cm ($1^1/_2$") cubes; place them in a bowl, add all the ingredients for the first marinade and rub into the chicken; marinate for 40 minutes; drain and squeeze out excess liquid from the chicken.
2. Mix all the ingredients for the second marinade and rub into the chicken; marinate for 30 minutes.
3. Mix the breadcrumbs and sesame seeds in a plate; roll the chicken pieces in this mixture and refrigerate for 15 minutes.
4. Heat the oil in a wok, *karhai,* deep-fry the chicken pieces, a few at a time, on medium heat for 3 to 4 minutes or until done; remove and drain; serve hot with mint-coriander chutney (see p. 12).

COOK'S NOTE
Prawns can be used in place of chicken cubes.

Amritsari Fried Fish

PREPARATION TIME: 15 MINUTES
MARINATING TIME: 50 MINUTES
COOKING TIME: 20 MINUTES
SERVES 4

750 g fish fillets

For the first marinade:
1/2 cup vinegar
1 tbsp salt

For the second marinade:
2 tbsp ginger paste
2 tbsp garlic paste
2 tsp carom seeds (*ajwain*)
1 tsp white pepper
1/2 tsp salt
1/2 cup gram flour (*besan*)
a few drops orange food colour
1/2 cup water

oil to deep-fry
lemon wedges to garnish

1. Wash the fish fillets, pat dry with paper towels and cut into even-sized cubes or fingers; place them in a bowl, rub in the vinegar and salt and marinate for 30 minutes; drain and pat dry again with paper towels.
2. Mix all the ingredients for the second marinade, rub into the fish and marinate for 20 minutes.
3. Heat the oil in a wok, *karhai*, deep-fry the fish pieces a few at a time over medium heat until crisp; remove and drain; arrange on a platter, garnish with lemon wedges and serve hot.

Panna Summer Drink

PREPARATION TIME: 10 MINUTES
COOKING TIME: 10 MINUTES
SERVES 4

400 g unripe mangoes

1 litre (4 cups) water
250 g sugar
1 tsp dry-roasted cumin powder (see p. 12)
1 tsp dry mint, powdered
salt to taste
1/4 tsp black salt

1. Peel the mangoes, place in a pressure cooker along with 1 cup water and pressure cook for 7 to 8 minutes, or boil till the mangoes are soft; cool; mash the pulp and discard the seeds; pass the pulp through a sieve to get a smooth consistency.
2. Put the pulp in a jug, add the remaining water, sugar, cumin powder, mint, salt and black salt and stir; if the *panna* is too thick, add more water; serve chilled.

Thandai Milk Drink

PREPARATION TIME: 15 MINUTES
SOAKING TIME: 5 – 6 HOURS
SERVES 4

125 g sugar
3 cups water
20 almonds, blanched, peeled
1 tsp aniseed (*saunf*)
5-6 rose petals
5-6 peppercorns
2 tbsp melon seeds (*magaz*)
3-4 cardamoms
a few strands saffron
$2\frac{1}{2}$ cups milk

1. Put the sugar and $1\frac{1}{2}$ cups water in a pan and boil to make a thin syrup; cool and reserve.
2. Put the remaining water in a bowl and add the almonds, aniseed, rose petals, peppercorns, melon seeds, cardamoms and saffron and soak for 5 to 6 hours; transfer to a blender and grind till smooth.
3. Transfer the almond mixture to a jug, add the syrup and the milk and stir well; serve the *thandai* chilled in tall glasses.

ABOUT THE AUTHORS

The Members of the External Affairs [Ministry's] Spouses Association (EASA), based in New Delhi, have put together the recipes for this book, selecting the best from the Association's own collection developed over many years by generations of EASA Members. From right to left: President, Mrs. Anita Saran, who spearheaded the project; Vice-President, Mrs. Sunita Ahmed, who opened her home for the photography sessions; Savita Mudgal, Padma Akbaruddin and Kiran Sachdev who cooked the food. Many other members gave valuable assistance to the Cookbook Team.

Other titles in this series include:

- Quick Meals by Tannie Baig
- The Best of South-East Asian Cuisine by Tannie Baig
- Soups ◆ Salads ◆ Crêpes by Tannie Baig
- Dishes with Fishes by Tannie Baig
- Low Fat Sampler by Tannie Baig
- Egg(x)travaganza by Tannie Baig
- Choicest Indian Curries by Tannie Baig
- Vegetarian Special by Tannie Baig
- Delectable Desserts and Puddings by Tannie Baig
- Cooking with Herbs by Tannie Baig
- Indian Vegetarian Cuisine by Kikky Sihota
- Continental Cuisine for India by Kikky Sihota
- Fusion Food: Vegetarian Special by Komal Taneja
- Fusion Food: Non-Vegetarian Special by Komal Taneja
- The Power of Potatoes by Komal Taneja
- Mughlai Cooking at Home by Komal Taneja
- Fabulous Flavours: Non-Vegetarian by EASA
- Fabulous Flavours: Vegetarian by EASA